Copyright © 2012 by Jay Media Publishing

All rights reserved. Printed in the United States of America
No part of this book may be reproduced, stored in a retrieval system, or transmitted by any means, electronic, mechanical, photocopying, recording or otherwise, without the express written permission of the copyright holder.

www.princessandpartner.com

ISBN 978-0-9849290-0-9

Written by Dion Johnson, Jr and Christione Johnson
Written assistance by Dion and Christine Johnson

Illustrations by Yasenia D. Maye

All through the week as they slumber
Daddy's little children often wonder
All about the Letter "A"
And this is how they start their day:
"Rise and shine let's go find dad
And tell him all about the lovely dreams we've had!"

"Good morning children,
SUNDAY starts our week,
About your dream, who wants to speak?"

Daddy's little princess puts her hand in the air,
"I will be the first to share!"

"I was in a swamp with my heavy friend
With a long tail and scaly green skin.
We wanted to swim but Mom said, 'Later'
So I had to leave the friendly...

"I was at the circus and up in the sky
These guys were swinging and flying high.
One swooshed down low and took my hat,
Then she laughed, that silly ...

"An acrobat came down and took your hat?
I can't believe that she did that!"

"To get it back in your dreams tonight,
You must go to bed and get tucked in real tight."

"Good morning children, aren't you glad?
It's TUESDAY so tell me all about the dream you've had."

"Daddy's little princess beamed with pride.
I dreamt about a springtime ride."

"On our way to church and what did I see
Stretching high in the sky but a tall fruit tree.
I wanted a treat to eat before chapel
So we stopped to get a shiny, red...

"Good morning children, we're halfway there. It's WEDNESDAY now, any dreams to share?"

Daddy's little partner was so excited that He blurted out his dream, he couldn't hold back

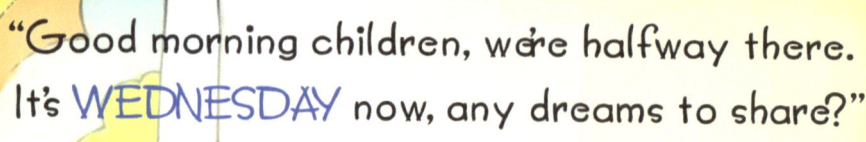

"While visiting a pet store I saw
Talking dogs, walking fish and flying frogs.
This was such a sight, I could not resist
I had to paint it 'cause I was an...

"An artist — that sounds grand,
But talking dogs and fish that stand?"

"Flying frogs, that's a crazy sight.
Let's see what fills your dreams tonight."

"I was in a restaurant up in a cloud
Daddy's little partner was also in the crowd.
He looked and saw his laces in a tangle
So I flew over to help 'cause I was an...

"An angel, was that a dream or reality?
Because you are always an angel to me."

"Lie down and close your eyes real tight
Maybe you'll have another angelic night."

"Good morning children, FRIDAY is here.
The last day of school, the weekend is near."

Daddy's little partner jumped up high
"You must first hear about my tale from the sky."

"I was on the moon and saw this guy
In a funny car driving by
With his friend, a space robot
They were exploring, I think he's an...

"You saw an astronaut in outer space?
How did you get to such a far place?"

"Can you come back down, it's getting dark
In your bed is where you must park."

"Good morning children, it's SATURDAY
It's time for cartoons, games and play."

Daddy's little partner and princess beamed bright
"Dad, tell us about the dream you had last night!"

"My dream was filled with people I knew
My little partner, princess and Mommy were there too.

We were talking and laughing
— things we love to do.

And then I woke up and found my dream had come true!"

Meet the Authors:
Dion Johnson, Jr. & Christione Johnson

Dion Johnson, Jr is a 7 year old second grader who likes to play soccer, board games and Pokemon. He also likes to draw and his favorite subject in school is math. Since he enjoys reading books, he loved being able to write his own. He would like to thank the illustrator and his mom and dad for helping them start writing the book and he would like to thank his sister for her good ideas.

Christione Johnson is a 6 year old first grader who likes to dance, play the Wii and board games. Her favorite subject in school is math. Her favorite part about writing this book was being able to figure out words that rhyme with one another. She would like to thank her mom and dad and the illustrator for helping with the book and she would like to thank her brother for his good ideas and for working with her to make this book.